CORGI BOOKS

THE GOLDEN RULES OF GOLF

A CORGI BOOK 0 552 12593 8

First publication in Great Britain

PRINTING HISTORY
Corgi edition published 1985
Corgi edition reissued 1985

Corgi Books are published by Transworld Publishers Ltd.,
Century House, 61-63 Uxbridge Road, Ealing, London W5 5SA,
in Australia by Transworld Publishers (Aust.) Pty. Ltd.,
26 Harley Crescent, Condell Park, NSW 2200, and in New
Zealand by Transworld Publishers (N.Z.) Ltd., Cnr. Moselle
and Waipareira Avenues, Henderson, Auckland.

Made and printed in Great Britain by
Hunt Barnard Printing Ltd., Aylesbury, Bucks.

The Player must play the game with integrity and honesty at all times.

Long grass and bushes may be moved only to enable a Player to find and identify a ball that is lying among them.

The Player shall be courteous to all other players on the course at all times.

The ball shall be played as it lies except as otherwise provided for in the Rules or Local Rules.

It is advisable to play in clothes which do not restrict movement.

The Player shall have five minutes in which to find a 'lost' ball.

8

Partners may share clubs provided that the total number of clubs carried by the side does not exceed fourteen.

The Player shall use one ball only during each game or match, unless the ball is lost.

The Club Professional is always willing to help, advise and guide the Player on any aspect of the game.

When a competition is played over an extended period, the Committee shall lay down the limit of time within which each round shall be completed.

Except as provided for under the Rules, the Player shall not use any artificial device which might assist him in making a stroke or in his play.

The Player must be careful when walking near to or on the practice range.

No Player should play until the players in front are out of range.

The Player can only replace those clubs which are broken accidentally.

If the ball is believed to be lying in water in a water hazard the Player may probe for it with a club or otherwise.

The Player shall not play while his ball is moving.

If a ball lies on a putting green other than that of the hole being played, the player shall lift the ball and drop it at a determined point.

The Player may carry and use up to fourteen clubs.

When dropping a ball the Player must fact towards the hole and drop it over his shoulder.

The Player shall not make undue noise whilst his opponent is playing.

If you cannot get to a course as often as you would like, it is useful to practise at home.

Any movable obstruction may be removed. If the ball be moved in so doing, it shall be replaced on the exact spot from which it was moved, without penalty.

No Player or caddie shall take any action to influence the position or the movement of a ball except in accordance with the Rules.

The Player shall not discontinue play on account of bad weather or for any reason, unless he considers that there be danger from lightning.

When the Player has played a stroke and the ball is of danger to other persons, he shall shot 'Fore!' as by way of a warning.

The Player shall not stand close behind another player who is making a stroke.

If a ball lying in casual water, ground under repair or a hole cast or runway made by a burrowing animal, a reptile or a bird, is not visible, the Player may probe for it.

A good firm grip of your club is essential for every type of stroke.

The Player is not the sole judge as to whether his ball is unfit for play.

In Match Play, if a Player's ball be stopped or deflected by himself, his partner or either of their caddies or equipment, he shall lose the hole.

The Player may move sand, loose soil or any loose
impediments on the putting green by picking them
up or brushing them aside.

The Player may not willingly upset an opponent in any way whilst playing.

'Out of Bounds' is ground on which any play is prohibited.

The Player shall at all times play without delay. Between the completion of a hole and driving off the next tee, the Player may not delay play in any way.

The Player is advised not to practise any strokes in
very windy conditions.

If the Player's opponent is lost and is not found after five minutes, a new opponent can be used.

Each Player is allowed one caddie only.

From the first teeing ground the ball may be played from the ground, from a heap of sand, or from a wooden or plastic tee.

Local Notices regulating the movement of golf cars should be strictly observed.

When playing a competition the Player shall start at the time and the order arranged by the Committee.

A Player may not try to improve his shot by removing, bending or breaking anything that is fixed or growing.

The ball shall be fairly struck at with the head of the club and must not be pushed, scraped or spooned.

If the Player plays a stroke and misses the ball, he shall count it as a stroke and play again.

If two competitors disagree on a point of play during a competition, they shall ask the referee for a decision and not resolve it themselves.

The Player may not hit the ball twice.